Firesmoke

Poems

Sheniz Janmohamed

TSAR

We acknowledge the support of the Canada Council for the Arts for our publishing program. We also acknowledge support from the Government of Ontario through the Ontario Arts Council.

We acknowledge the financial support of the Government of Canada through the Canada Book Fund for our publishing activities

Canada Council for the Arts Conseil des Arts du Canada ONTARIO ARTS COUNCIL CONSEIL DES ARTS DE L'ONTARIO Canadä

Cover photo by Shivankur Sharma
Cover design by Nadiya Virani

The following poems have been previously published:

"A Bluebird's Wing" in *West Coast Line*, #72, Winter 2012; and in *Catamaran Literary Reader*, Issue 3, June 2013
"Occupy" in *West Coast Line*, #72, Winter 2012
"Ajmer" in *South Asian Ensemble*, Autumn 2014
"Of Waves and Women" in *Wordspell Anthology*, September 2014
"Unleashed" in *From the Root*, Issue 1, August 2014

Library and Archives Canada Cataloguing in Publication

Janmohamed, Sheniz, author
Firesmoke / Sheniz Janmohamed.

Poems.
ISBN 978-1-927494-42-4 (pbk.)

1. Ghazals, Canadian. I. Title.

PS8619.A6764F57 2014 C811'.6 C2014-902554-8

Printed and bound in Canada by Coach House Printing

TSAR Publications
P. O. Box 6996, Station A
Toronto, Ontario M5W 1X7
www.tsarbooks.com

Be charitable like the river,
generous like the sun,
hospitable like the earth.

—KHWAJA MUINUDDIN CHISHTI

(of Ajmer)

Contents

Preface

When a fire is extinguished, ashes fall and smoke ascends. Smoke becomes one with the wind, sky, and air. Ashes are absorbed by the soil, land, and earth.

What happens to fire when it no longer exists?

Writing *Firesmoke* was like playing with fire. Nothing went according to plan. I couldn't make sense of what I was writing; it was ineffable. Every time I re-read these poems, I was left with a lightness, an airiness, an inability to pin them down. When a poet chooses a title for a book, she also summons what it entails. Fire, after all, is a source of both creation (forging) and destruction. One cannot be separated from the other because they are both informed by each other. As a result, the title of the book harkens to the relationship between fire and smoke by placing the words next to each other. There is no telling when fire will turn to smoke—when life will transform into death.

In order to write these poems, I had to locate, gather and lay down the kindling of my past—my attachments and fears—and watch them burn. I had to let go of my idea of what the future would hold and watch it disappear like smoke. The only presence that was present was the life of the fire itself.

But fire does not burn without being stoked.

BOOK STRUCTURE:

KINDLING	*FIRE*	*SMOKE*
ghazals	*free verse*	*short verse*

Pilgrimage

I have been in your presence many times before, walked barefoot through your dusty gullies. You have been the echoing azaan[1] in my heart, that mirror where I polish my reflection. How long has it been since I've seen you? Centuries? You haven't changed, except for the madness of those around you. They have become less mad and more maddening. But you, the pearl in this ramshackle desert, you shine like a shard of moonlight captured on earth. A thousand roses cannot rival the scent of one rose plucked from your fields. Khwaja makes them sweeter, turning pieces of coal to tinted blooms. If they could bleed, they'd drip sweet syrup, enough to quench the thirst of all the beggars in your streets. Ajmer roses drain themselves of their glory to throw themselves on your tomb, their heads bowing to you with white petals.

The rich, the famous, they come to you with envelopes stuffed with lakhs, bribes to keep their faces plastered on billboards. But the true pil grim is the common pigeon, who offers his last feather at your feet. Naked and free from the weight of his feathers, now he can fly.

I circled this shrine seven times when I was her. Someone I knew as myself once. My eyelashes were her eyelashes, curled from bending upwards to honour the sun. We are the same spirit, braiding our hair with the thorns of your discarded roses. Our scratches bear the names of who we were, the symbols of our sacrifices. She is the one in your morning mist, writhing in the sunlight. She is the sand in the strained voices of the *qawwals*, who tap their *dholaks* in your praise. She is the swirling spiral of incense under your emerald *chaddor*.

She goes by the name Israh, and I am her mere shadow, tugging at the *pallu* of her sari.

Pilgrim, watch your step. Her heart lies at the gate of this *dargah*.[2]

1 call to prayer

2 sufi shrine

I

KINDLING

Ah!

These ashes, the remains of a flame that once stoked the fire within Israh.
Even in its absence, the spark is ever present. Emptiness takes form in Israh.

Darkness descends. How will she find the kindling for the sacred fire of her heart?
The acacia offers its thorns. Gathering the bark of her fear, Israh sets fire to Israh.

These thorns prick her wrists as she writes, smearing the page with proof of life.
Each word is the petrified wood of memory, blowing breath into the lungs of Israh.

How do you awaken a warrior asleep in the cave of your heart? Sign her name.
As she wakes, your tears smudge her letters. All that remains is her sigh: ah!

A Bluebird's Wing

Geese fly back before the snow falls. January is the new spring.
If April is the cruelest month, how can winter rival an eternal spring?

With words etched into his skin, he extracts letters from his fingers.
She fans herself with his love letter, folded like a bluebird's wing.

The crow is the keeper of the Sacred Law, but you deem it evil.
If one crow is the ink of death, what will a murder of crows bring?

Steamrollers flatten the soil. Fish bones are coated with bitumen.
What melody will our rivers remember if songbirds forget how to sing?

Every Street Dog Should Have a Name

Cowering in a corner riddled with beetlenut spit,this street dog should have a name.
Wandering the gullies, bellies growing, every street dog should have a name.

Sleeping under autorickshaws and chauffeured cars, their beds never the same.
Who cares, They're just dogs. Perhaps you'd care if every street dog had your name.

The coiffed ones, with rhinestone collars, are pictured in fancy frames.
A mutt with red eyes and a bruised paw: a mere street dog with no name.

Dogs are descendants of wolves: their snarls signal that fame.
Howling annoyed sleepers awake: *We are street dogs with no names.*

What is this life but laboured mortality? Nothing remains but a name.
If a name will save it a kick, let every street dog take my name.

Occupy

Without a blank canvas, what can art occupy?
In emptiness, they bring form to occupy.

You're a blind man searching the dirt for keys.
There are no more rooms in this heart to occupy.

They broke the back of this land.
How many trees did they break apart to occupy?

Her trembling fingers rummage through an empty wallet.
Shivering in the darkness of her tent, she starts to #occupy.

Heretic

Your heart is as empty as a grave, so why not blame a heretic?
Heresy remains with those who point to blame a heretic.

She's chosen madness and reason over reason and madness.
She answers to no one, not even herself. Who can tame a heretic?

Crouched in a cave, his face ashen with the white flame of death.
Naked as a child before birth, how can you shame a heretic?

Leaving the mosque, she found salvation in a handful of red soil.
Rubbing its vermillion on her forehead, Israh is named a heretic.

Unleashed

They believed a witch unleashed a storm when she loosened her hair.
How many hurricanes have hurled through towns because of your hair?

Leaning against a traffic light, a ragged street doll clasps her hands together.
A couple of coins will never rinse the pain out from her dirt-streaked hair.

Each strand of her hair is silk spun from the night. She will never tie it.
She tells me her power is not in her hands, lips, eyes. It's in her hair.

Her glance is an arrow cracking the oak of your heart.
Even thunder whispers when Israh unties her hair.

Draupadi of Delhi

for Jyoti Singh Pandey

You are our reflection, ripping the veils from this mirror of injustice.
Never able to eat again, you are always hungry, hungry for justice.

A nameless name, a hoarse cry penetrating the depths of our wombs.
We will shake ourselves loose from the chains of this corrupted 'justice'.

Our Draupadi of Delhi, they tried to unravel the sari of your spirit, but failed.
This rage is a flame that spreads into an inexhaustible fire: We demand justice.

They place wreaths at the feet of goddesses and then kick us in the streets.
Israh invokes Durga Ma: Destroy demons with your sword of justice!

Kali Ma

Break the bones in the body: The body that breaks the bones of women.
Your black milk flows into the mouths of men who dare to trample women.

Queen of the night: you have birthed dusk from dawn, coal from diamond.
You carry the weight of life, breathing fire into the breasts of women.

Your trident is our spine. Your hue is the bottomless ocean in our wombs.
Every strand of your hair is a quill, pricking the wells in the hearts of women.

Oh, three-eyed warrior, fierce and loving. You see everything beyond sight.
Your necklace clanks with skulls. You are the Dark Mother in all women.

We embrace your ebony shadow. Our skin gleams black, like hematite.
Bleeding with rage and renewal, we rewrite stories men have written for women.

Change your clothes. Keep your eyes down. Stop tempting men with your looks.
We reject poison from their foaming mouths: tar that once stuck to the ribs of women.

Kali Ma, your tongue hangs from our tongues. We refuse to keep our mouths shut.
Israh will scream until her throat burns: *We were not born simply to woo men!*

The Crone

A raven ruffles its feathers but cannot shake off the night.
The language of the birds, sacred and unknown, speaks to me.

This past is a skeleton unburied in the dust of a forgotten desert.
I sift through the sand, and every blanched bone speaks to me.

She cuts into the tree of my being, revealing the rings of my life.
Unbroken circles that never touch, like stones that speak to me.

Eyes glaze with the sheen of the sea, wrinkles are tributaries of tears.
Come to the edge, Israh. I am the crone who speaks to me.

Before Spring

Snowflakes fluttering from the clouds like white blossoms.
Each dissolves upon touch: where impermanence blossoms.

A nun kneels down to plant bulbs by the foot of a cherry tree.
Cartwheels of prayer skip through the street: pink blossoms.

If rain swept itself across the hearts of city dwellers,
How many seeds would perish and how many would blossom?

Branches frozen, an willow is stunned between frost and sunlight.
Weaving words like vines, Israh offers you this wreath of blossoms.

Spring

Your breath in mine, my breath in yours. You have taught me how to breathe again.
Inhaling you like the forest inhales sunlight— gold before darkness descends again.

Come to the garden, I have scattered new seeds and torn out the weeds of our past.
Your love blooms like gardenia, lilac and jasmine. Spring has found itself again.

I've killed and revived our love as many times as these kohl-rimmed eyes have blinked.
If we keep our eyes open to the reality of death, will our love survive annihilation again?

My beloved's shrine is lit with four lamps. To be the fifth, my heart sets itself ablaze.
These feet stomp soil and rain into mud— Israh has learned how to dance again.

Laila

In this state of madness, I have no one else to blame
I become the fire, the flame, the letters in your name.

My hair is tangled and I have lost reason and shame
I become the fire, the flame, the letters in your name.

Am I the target of your love? Here's an arrow, take aim.
I become the fire, the flame, the letters in your name.

Forbidden to see his beloved Laila, Majnun still came.
He became the fire, the flame, the letters in her name.

Turning On the Heels of This Love

Turning around the axis of the earth, she spins the wheel of this love.
Others sit like stagnant water, questioning the appeal of this love.

Even the swimmer will struggle against the waves of the sea.
Surrender to its rhythm and drown! What more can you feel of this love?

Dig the soil and rubble of your being, seek until the madness finds you.
This box contains the secret of your secret. Open it. Break the seal of this love!

She finds Khizr in the forest of her heart, her robes drenched with mud.
Whirling into leaves and wind, Israh turns on the heels of this love.

II

FIRE

Embracing Darkness

Darkness,
you terrified me.

The shapes you twisted into,
shadows folding within shadows
open mouths with no faces

You were that hallowed emptiness
I couldn't bear to peer into
an endless tunnel into a black hole
of silence

So I slept in
the soft glow of a bedside lamp
protecting myself
from your grasp.

But you are present
in the onyx of my curls
the dark sheen of my eyes

You are a wound
the tree of my being will leave behind

A womb to plant new seeds.

I leaned into you
when I could no longer stand
and you cradled me
with the arms of Kali Ma

your soot
became my starlight.

I navigated through you
after every light faded
except the one in my heart.

I walked with you
through the forest, the trees bending their heads
like dervishes swaying back and forth
into breath

I sat with you
on a sand-riddled bench
staring into you
as you spread like a blot of ink
pooling itself on paper

I gazed
until I no longer saw

my hands, feet, legs

the cabins, leaves, pebbles,

the pixels of light
in the distance.

A hermit in the cave of darkness
I became you
embracing myself.

Letting Go

Your mouth open
like a gaping oyster
a pearl exposed,
plucked from your heart.

As we witness your stillness
we face our own inevitability.

I wait

for your
eyes to open

for your
hands to twitch

But you are not there

As we mutter prayers
over you, or what was you

we weave each syllable around ourselves

Protection to face
what cannot be faced
but what cannot be avoided

Like a mirror
staring back at us.

Just a few days ago
I touched your fuzzy head,

and you fell
in and out of sleep
murmuring *I love you*
and *Who's that?*
every time someone walked in the room.

after I read you Buddha's words,
I walked barefoot into the sunshine,
crouched by the light-dappled pool
Eyes following the film
of dead petals skimming the surface,
surrendering to the ebb of water.

I submerged my toes
in its coolness
Knowing you would never again
experience
the shudder and delight
of freezing water.

Stoking the Fire

Stumbling out of the tent,
I look up and the shock of the stars
makes me forget, for a moment,
the ice in my breath
my socks drenched with dew

If I were any closer to the fire,
I'd be burning with it.
And in the morning,
the ashes still smouldering,
the ground grey with soot,
I sit on the edge of a worn log
gaze into the dying flames
and wonder
how to stoke the mind's fire.

Walking Meditation

In this darkness
the grass
damp with dew,
glistens under
a star-flecked sky.

The wet blades graze
my shins.

We walk in a circle
eyes down, chins tucked in
hands folded in front at the solar plexus.

One foot after the other
one foot
after
the other
one
foot after
the other
one foot after
the other

concentrate
too
much
and
I'll trip over my own feet

act too casual and
I'll trip
someone else.

one foot after the other,
that is all.

The ground wet
and solid beneath
our boots

And yet, with each huff of breath,
with each measured step,
we know
this earth is only as solid
as we are.

Here

We sit
across from each other
eyes down, ears pricked

Our bowls
abundant with lettuce,
tomatoes, cucumbers
avocado dressing.

We break bread
in the most fulfilling meal of our lives
and share it without speaking

The air is absent of human voices,
like breath under water
muted and amplified at once.

I want to tell you
I'm glad I'm here, with you.
Well, not with you, with myself.
I can't speak to you.
Why am I here again?
What is happening to me?
Is this really it?

I want to tell you
I'm here.

I am here, amidst the
stacking of plates,
pouring of hot tea,

footsteps, drumming,
birdsong, noise in my head.

Without looking, speaking, or touching,
you respond

I know.

Bottomless Tree

Grasping further
and further
into the core
of the earth

Only to be touched by fire
a deep burning
roots into flames
flames into ash.

Embrace

Your heart is
the origin of fire
pulsating in the core of the earth

the lava in your veins
has hardened to rock

a memory of what was once volcanic

Walk yourself into the woods
self flagellate with willow branches

spin

until leaves weave themselves into your hair
until the hem of your skirt hangs with mud

Then
come to me
and I will embrace you

Each scar, each gash
a reminder of
who you
were

Roots

We come home,
    our hands sticky with sap
    our clothes heavy with the scent of firesmoke

Of the burning woods

    palo santo
        pine
    birch
        juniper
    cedar
        willow

we rub the ashes of tree trunks
on our chests
and declare ourselves
worshippers of roots

Roots so deep,
we pull them out by reaching into our chests.

Sapling

Sprouting from the womb of soil
your tendrils stretching towards
the orb of the sun
it casts its warm rays
over your gentle head.
Grow
be unafraid to reach the forest canopy
to see with your eyes
yellow birds
perching on your branches
eagles circling around your crown
your roots
spreading into the damp earth,
highways for tiny critters
journeying underground.
the rolling landscape of fellow trees
swaying
to the symphony of the forest.

And you too,
will let the wind bend you,
sweetening your sap
with its breath.

Kailash

Shake this ice from my shoulders
Let it melt into nectar
To fill the cup of your heart.

You can't climb the sacred jewel of Tibet,
the abode of Lord Shiva
you can only encircle it, your robes
sweeping the ground as you prostrate
and rise.

Each mountain face glints with
    crystal
    ruby
    lapis
    gold

the lotus of six mountain ranges
scatters white petals of snow
to the wind

They say the stairways of Kalaish
lead to paradise but
one foot
on the mountain step will send you
tumbling
down
into
death.

This mountain
need not be climbed
for you to reach its summit.

Kilimanjaro

Sit like a mountain.
Let the snow swirl around you
Let the world nest in the rock of your being

Wedged between earth and sky,
you watch over the city, breathing
over the madness, traffic, lights.
Clouds veil the curves of your face,
fog lingers at the crown of your head.
Someday you will crumble into
an avalanche, or sputter
sparks from your mouth.

In your hand, you hold the weight of a mountain.

A rock once belonged to a mountain,
A mountain that was once under the sea,
now at the height of the stars.

Close your palm and sit like Kilimanjaro.

Let the snow swirl around you
Let the world nest in the rock of your being.
Root yourself in this earth
and it will root itself in you.

Matka

I come to you with an offering:

a chunk of turquoise
to drop into the lake of your heart

breaking the skin of your labradorescence
sinking under fingers of algae
resting with moss-slick rocks.

Thunder summons the bloated sky
Tearing its belly open.

Each drop is
a rainbow suspended in quartz
a frozen prism shattering into circles.

drenched in rainsheen,

I come to you with an offering:

a clay pot to fill
until it overflows.

Mirror

The lake is still,
a mirror of silence.

The stars bow down
to drink from its depths
each drowning in its own reflection
watery pools of light.

Who can separate sky from water?

Only the blade of the horizon, tearing
through the union
scattering daylight, pushing the stars back
into obscurity.

As if they no longer existed.
As if they never did.

Tasbih

This bead
is a black hole
a starless night
my shadow
caving into itself.

This bead
is a full moon
A water opal
spinning circles
into the lake.

This bead
is a lump of clay
A terracotta pot
hardening in
the heat of a kiln.

This bead
is a hollowed oak
a mossy stump
claiming itself back
to the earth.

Winter Stone

If I crack you open,

Will you spin out into the Northern Lights
Or spill out like the sea?

Will your incandescence dissolve like mist
or stain my fingers with rainbow slicks?

You are
the golden sheen of moss after a rainfall
the cobalt flame in the breath of a fire
the sky mirrored in the bottom of a well

ice preserved in rock
rock encased in ice

A shapeshifter trapped in stone.

Of Waves and Women

The moon is the ultimate shapeshifter
A phantom glow
An ancient luminescence
Governing
The cycles of waves and women.

She blows into the conch shell,
her breath rippling
through the body of the ocean.

The ocean pours
saltwater rivers into her veins,
claiming her blood as its own.

Where does she end?
Where the waves begin.

Goddess

The moon is my only witness tonight.
She sits low on the horizon, communing
with the clouds.
She weaves the sun's radiance into her own,
surpassing it in grace.

She works her magic
while the world sleeps

summoning
dreamers, lunatics, lovers
to the edge of her being—

and then
she swallows us
whole.

In the Current

The child I was
is just one breath away

Stones skip across the river of who I was
and I acknowledge the resonance
without drowning
in who I should've been

In the current
Floating, sometimes sinking
Swallowing water
Sometimes a gulp of air.

Flotsam

beer bottles plastic bags underwear gum wrappers
receipts caps toothbrushes lighters cups

end up in the sea's vast net of light
waves heaving the weight of
our waste back and forth
back and forth

the ocean
tumbling shards of beer bottles
into oblong pebbles of sea glass
weaving bloated plastic bags
into nooses for seagulls
breaking bottle caps
into bait for lantern fish

Our sparkling garbage dump
brims with cockles and crap

Our hands throw
trash overboard

The giver of life receives.

The Ocean

I sit on the rock-riddled banks
of this river
as the current shifts with the breeze
and
water bubbles up and collapses into itself

You stand
on the other side
A blurred outline
in the mist
in the midst
of these tears.

If only I had a boat
If only I knew how to swim

I would pour myself into you

and
this
river
would
become an estuary.

Stones and Spirals

Stone by stone
we lay down spirals

life within life
death within death

A centre that unravels
turns into itself

A centre that never moves
yet always spins

Rooted in rock
and
swept away by a single wave.

Stone by stone
we lay down
  spirals.

Where the Road Bends

I have been where you stand
in the middle of the road
where windswept leaves
scatter russet patterns
on the pavement.

Asked the road to bend
so I can hide in its curve
so I can walk without being   seen.

Walking Stick

bent like my back,
its spine curls around my palm
its knot fits my hand, this walking stick.

Saint Patrick
ambled through Ireland
past emerald groves
and over verdant hills
rocks and across rivers
spreading the Gospel
until he rooted his walking stick in the ground,
and it bloomed
into an Ash tree.

Now, I'm no saint,
but think of all the forests there would be
if we stood still for a while,
and let our walking sticks
root themselves in the earth.

Watering the Seed

I have planted a bodhi seed in
the forest of my mind,
its soil rich with litterfall.

How long will it take for this tiny pod
to flower into a peepal tree,
under the shade of which
I will attain enlightenment?

As long as you water it,
it will grow.

Prayer Flags

Tattered prayer flags
hanging from a dilapidated balcony
writhing in the bitter winter wind
Blocks of colour
in a discarded corner of a drab
snow-dusted apartment block.

Even in this city, far from
the ice of the Himalayas,
prayers are whipped up in the air
trapped in wind tunnels
and released into the stone blue sky

Winter Approaches

A sumac bends over a frozen stream
Petrified by its own reflection.

The bough is sheathed in ice
and a fine dust of snow.

Each branch needles the overcast sky,
stunned into silence.

When the last leaf falls,
what will die within us?

Driftwood

for the beloved Musadiq Sanwal

Your voice was the boat
keeping me afloat
on the waters of my sleep

Now
it is driftwood
floating downstream.

Tell me,
did you drown with Khusrau?
did you reach the farther shore?

Sandalwood

They say
when you pass from this world
to the next
your senses disappear like smoke
the last one to leave is
that of scent.

I offer you

a vase of blooming tea roses
a scarf full of fresh lilacs
a brass bowl brimming with rose water
a handful of sticky acacia resin
a wedge of burning palo santo
a heap of dried lavender
a single leaf of white sage
a sprig of night jasmine

You will know my love
through spirals of sandalwood smoke.

Firesmoke

did you hear the words of the sufi
as he stepped into the fire

he spoke in a language
a language not known to those who listen
with their ears

He brought the sun to his lips
to taste ancient rivers of amber

his hands grasped burnt bark
smudging his face with blackened pine

until he could no longer be seen in this world

one with the tree that burns
crackling in the circle
the breath of the sun
exhaling between the clouds

firesmoke

III

SMOKE

Offering

The forest in my heart
is burning
to give way
for new growth.

Everything I am
has been thrown
into this sacred fire.

Set this heart ablaze
and breathe flames
into these lungs
for
what does not burn
cannot be destroyed.

Robin's Egg

Her heart is as delicate
as a robin's egg
An immaculate blue
like the sky scraped free
of clouds
With one nudge,
it cracks into sunlight

One Breath

How to forget you?
I'm only one breath away
And in that breath, life.

Gone

My past is
a heap of sand
a meteorite
a mountain reduced to dust

a sea cave
salt water lapping against my mouth
bile in the back of my throat.

Whistling Thorn

Plunging my hands
into the ground
soil digging under my fingernails
until I uncover my beating heart
its arteries
the roots of an acacia

These tears of rediscovery
are like stinging ants
boring holes into
my heart

A whistling thorn
hollow at its core

so the wind
can find music
in its emptiness

Between the Pines

muddied boots
frozen fingertips
her shawl dragging on the forest floor
dry leaves and twigs in its fraying edge
bellowing sage, breath, fresh air
firesmoke woven between strands of black curls

she could
stand
between these pines

and not be seen.

Weeping Willow

Regal and rooted
in your grief
and yet
when the breeze
catches your branches
you dance.

Truth

What do you know of truth?

I know it in my bones,
The way
trees know the wind.

Cardinal

A shock of crimson
in the hush
of falling snow

Crow

Night folding into flight
Coal streaking the sky
Embers once were flames

Curling Leaf

leaves curl into fire
and spit ash
the circles of life
in the flame of death

Golden

Amongst the green leaves
a sliver of crumpled gold,
radiant in death.

Rose

Just one sigh
of perfume
before turning to dust.

Petals

Petals don't ask
where to land

They just fall
with grace.

Acknowledgements

To all my teachers—past, present and future, seen and unseen, animate and inanimate—to the trees, the birds, the flowers and the soil.

Theodore Tsaousidis, for your wisdom and compassion. For holding up a mirror so I can see what cannot be unseen.

To Shiv, for your unconditional love and astounding kindness. For being my constant in a world of uncertainty. For being an example to others, including myself.

Mom, for tending to the garden of my life, allowing me to plant my own seeds and bloom. For reminding me of the beauty, resilience, grace and fierce strength mothers possess, and to own it.

Dad, for teaching me how to smile and laugh in the face of adversity and pain. For reminding me that despite the odds, life can and does go on. For your persistence and sense of adventure.

Uncle, for your sharp wit and intelligence, for your unyielding support, encouragement and belief in me.

Aleeza, for being tireless in your support, generosity and positivity, for putting up with my little sister antics and always showing up when I need you. For bringing joy and laughter into my life.

Janmohamed, Hajee, Pilarski and Sharma families.

Julie Mehta, your love, kindness and generosity of spirit have provided me with the courage I need to continue to write. I owe you so much.

Nurjehan Aziz and M G Vassanji for your guidance, honesty and continued faith in me.

Gustavo, for your ability to understand without speaking. For your quiet strength and tireless dedication.

I am lucky to have strong, intelligent, fearless, creative women in my life. Thank you for your support, advice and love—Anita Majumdar, Nadiya Virani, Whitney French, Rajie Kabli, Eisha Anum Hussain, Summer Pervez and Samantha Rodin.

Helen Argiro, for teaching me what it means to have tenacity.

John Ryerson, for your mentorship, support and expertise.

Elder O'Puck, for giving me the gift of fire. For reminding me of its sacredness and its power. For your silent and spoken support.